MOUNT ST. HELENS AND TOUTLE RIVER. The Toutle River Valley—a barren, steaming landscape of mud and debris following the eruption—has become a magnificently eroded landscape that has slowly been re-populated with mosses, grasses, wildflowers, shrubs, and trees. The forest, which was buried or swept away by the eruption of May 18, 1980, had itself regrown since the previous eruption. It is probably safe to assume that, given time, the same will occur again—both re-growth and destruction.

From the WISH YOU WERE HERE. POSTCARD BOOK—Mount St. Helens

SIERRA PRESS

Phto ©Jim Hughes/Photo Venture

ROOSEVELT ELK. Although an estimated 1,500 elk were killed by the eruption, within days survivors from beyond the impacted area began to wander back. Their tracks and droppings helped speed the recovery of vegetation. Many mammals—like pocket gophers and golden-mantled ground squirrels—survived the blast because they were insulated beneath snow banks or were in their below-ground dens. These burrowing mammals have aided the regrowth of vegetation by digging up fertile soil from beneath the new, relatively sterile, volcanic ash and depositing it on the surface. Many biologists refer to them as the unsung heroes of the recovery process.

From the WISH YOU WERE HERE® POSTCARD BOOK—Mount St. Helens

SIERRA PRESS

Photo ©Jim Quiring

BLOWN DOWN TREES NORTH OF SPIRIT LAKE. Dense, black, ground-hugging clouds of steam and rock released by the eruption swept over four major ridges and valleys, reaching as far as 17 miles from their source. Wind speeds in these blast clouds reached a maximum of several hundred miles-per-hour and attained temperatures as great as 500° Fahrenheit. Close to the crater, 500-year-old trees, 6 feet in diameter, were uprooted and blown away. Following the eruption trees were blown down or snapped off, their trunks pointing downwind—away from Mount St. Helens. At greater distances, the blast slowed and gravity pulled the heavier-than-air clouds into down-valley twists and swirls. The outer limit of the devastated area is marked by a forest of dead trees. These trees were far enough removed from the eruption to remain standing, but were still killed by the searing heat of the blast.

From the WISH YOU WERE HERE≋ POSTCARD BOOK—Mount St. Helens

SIERRA PRESS

Photo ©Ed Cooper

FOREST ALONG THE TRAIL OF TWO FORESTS. While no lava flowed from the mountain during the eruption of May 18, 1980—there is stunning evidence on the south side of the mountain of past eruptions where large volumes of lava flowed down the mountain's sides. At both Ape Cave and The Trail of Two Forests, one walks through a forest that is growing on a 2,000-year-old lava flow. This basaltic lava is similar to the "quiet" Hawaiian eruptions of smooth pahoehoe lava. Although soils develop slowly on the hard surface of these flows, after 2,000 years the forest has been successful in its struggle to grow.

From the WISH YOU WERE HERE... POSTCARD BOOK—Mount St. Helens

SIERRA PRESS

Photo ©Jeff Nicholas

Scientist studying lava dome in Mount St. Helens' crater (early 1980s.) Geologists continue to monitor the lava dome in Mount St. Helens' crater. Here, gases are collected and analyzed, composition of newly formed rock is studied, and seismographs and tilt-meters provide valuable data to help scientists forecast how this volcano, and others, may behave in the future. Many answers have been discovered, but more questions than answers still remain. Geologists studying the history of Mount St. Helens have concluded that in the last 50,000 years the mountain has had at least 20 major, and countless minor, eruptions.

From the WISH YOU WERE HERE® POSTCARD BOOK—Mount St. Helens

SIERRA PRESS

Photo ©Gary Braasch

WATERFALL ON PINE CREEK, LAVA CANYON. Mudflows on the south side of the mountain were not as massive as on the north side. These mudflows, created when the heat of the eruption melted snow and ice from the mountain's sides, scoured some areas—like Lava Canyon—and covered others with layers of mud and rocks—as at Lahar. In Lava Canyon the mudflows carved new channels and waterfalls for the now gently melting snows of Mount St. Helens.

From the WISH YOU WERE HERE® POSTCARD BOOK—Mount St. Helens

SIERRA PRESS

Photo ©Jeff Nicholas

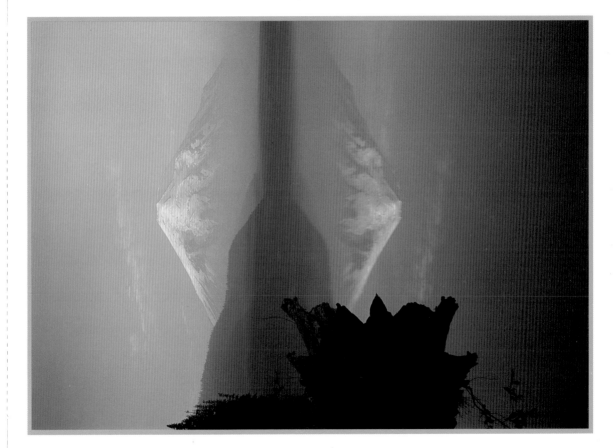

MOUNT ST. HELENS BEFORE THE ERUPTION OF MAY 18, 1980. In legend the mountain was known as Loowit—Lady of Fire. The volcano was first known as an ugly witch and then as a beautiful maiden; we know her today as Mount St. Helens. The changing volcanic activity of the peak over the past 4,000 years was probably the basis for the transformation in legend from burning witch to sleeping beauty and back again—a cycle that has been repeated many times over the centuries.

From the WISH YOU WERE HERE® POSTCARD BOOK—Mount St. Helens

SIERRA PRESS

Photo ©Ed Cooper

Douglas fir and lupine near Lahar. On the south side of the mountain—at Lahar (an Indonesian word for mudflow)—clay, rock, and debris have been deposited by mudflows created by melting snow and ice. Conifers, whose seeds are usually too heavy to be windblown, have been slower to return than wildflowers and shrubs. Nevertheless, lone individuals (like these Douglas firs) have found their way back. The recovery of this once barren landscape has taught biologists much about the process of natural recovery following a major environmental disruption.

From the WISH YOU WERE HERE® POSTCARD BOOK—Mount St. Helens

SIERRA PRESS

Photo ©Jack Dykinga

MOUNT ST. HELENS AND BLASTED TREES ON WINDY RIDGE. The view from Windy Ridge, on the eastern side of the Monument, provides a close-up view of much of the huge, open crater of Mount St. Helens. Here, in the heart of the eruption area, natural processes are being allowed to proceed without human interference. Researchers estimate it will take at least a century before these areas will be re-forested. It is entirely possible that someday a new summit cone will fill this huge crater. Perhaps, in a thousand years (or ten thousand?) Mount St. Helens and its surroundings will resemble what was here prior to its eruption that fateful morning in 1980.

From the WISH YOU WERE HERE® POSTCARD BOOK—Mount St. Helens

SIERRA PRESS

Photo ©Larry Ulrich

MOUNT ST. HELENS FROM JOHNSTON RIDGE OBSERVATORY. Located at the terminus of the 52-mile Spirit Lake Memorial Highway, Johnston Ridge Observatory provides spectacular views of the still-steaming lava dome, crater, pumice plain, and landslide deposits. The observatory, located only five miles from the mountain, was named in honor of David A. Johnston, a volcanologist for the U.S. Geological Survey who lost his life during the eruption of Mount St. Helens. He had been stationed at the Coldwater II observation post on Coldwater Ridge (re-named Johnston Ridge following the eruption) in roughly the same location as the observatory which bears his name. Johnston was one of the fifty-seven people who lost their lives in the eruption.

From the WISH YOU WERE HERE® POSTCARD BOOK—Mount St. Helens

SIERRA PRESS

Photo ©Jim Quiring

COLDWATER LAKE AND MOUNT ST. HELENS. While the eruption of Mount St. Helens altered (some would say destroyed) the old landscape, it also created a new one at the same time. Coldwater Lake, near the end of Spirit Lake Highway, did not exist prior to the eruption. The great avalanche of mud and debris that swept down the Toutle River Valley on the north side of the mountain dammed Coldwater Creek. Water backing up behind this debris dam formed the new lake. Castle Lake, on the other side of the valley, was formed in the same fashion.

From the WISH YOU WERE HERE® POSTCARD BOOK—Mount St. Helens

SIERRA PRESS

Photo ©Jeff Nicholas

Fireweed blooming near Ryan Lake. Despite early concerns about whether the forest environment would, or even could, recover, within weeks of the eruption fireweed, pearly everlasting, thistle, and blackberry had already reappeared. Within a year, a carpet of fireweed covered the thin ash layers near Ryan Lake on the north side of the Monument. Spread by wind, the small seeds of this hardy flower make it an ideal early colonizer in burned or disturbed areas.

From the WISH YOU WERE HERE® POSTCARD BOOK—Mount St. Helens

SIERRA PRESS

Photo ©Robert W. Decker/U.S. Geological Survey

MOUNT RAINIER, SPIRIT LAKE, AND DOME WITHIN MOUNT ST. HELENS' CRATER. Within Mount St. Helens' crater a dome of viscous lava squeezed up over the main vent, its red-hot interior exposed through cracks in the expanding surface. Several domes formed, and were blown out, during the summer of 1980. After that, a new dome grew in pulses (without disruption) until it reached its present height of more than 1,000 feet. Seen from the crater's southern rim, Mt. Rainier (50-miles distant) stands as a reminder of what once was, and, perhaps, of what will be.

From the WISH YOU WERE HERE® POSTCARD BOOK—Mount St. Helens

SIERRA PRESS

Photo ©Ed Cooper

MOUNT ST. HELENS ERUPTING, JULY 22, 1980. The small, but spectacular, eruption of Mount St. Helens on July 22, 1980, reminded the public and geologists alike that Mother Nature calls the tunes. Will Mount St. Helens erupt again? Yes! When? That remains to be seen.

From the WISH YOU WERE HERE™ POSTCARD BOOK—Mount St. Helens

SIERRA PRESS

Photo © Katia Krafft